SUMMARY
of
YOUNGER NEXT
YEAR

A FastReads Summary with Key Takeaways & Analysis

NOTE: The purpose of this FastReads summary is to help you decide if it's worth the time, money and effort reading the original book (if you haven't already). FastReads has pulled out the essence with commentary and critique—but only to help you ascertain the value of the book for yourself. This summary is meant to be a supplement to, and not a replacement for the original book.

Follow **this link** to purchase a copy of the original book on Amazon.

TABLE OF CONTENTS

EXECUTIVE SUMMARY 4

PART ONE TAKE CHARGE OF YOUR BODY 5

PART TWO TAKE CHARGE OF YOUR LIFE 13

KEY TAKEAWAYS 16

EDITORIAL REVIEW...20

ABOUT THE AUTHORS...22

EXECUTIVE SUMMARY

In their book *Younger Next Year: Live Strong, Fit, and Sexy—Until You're 80 and Beyond*, Chris Crowley and Henry S. Lodge explore the science-backed rules readers can use to reverse what is accepted as normal aging and grow functionally younger in the next five to ten years.

Crowley and Lodge draw a line between the natural and normal process of aging and the abnormal and dreadful process of decay. They reiterate that in the absence of signals to grow, the body will default to decay. The key to growth, they observe, is to exercise six days a week, eat healthy, and connect and commit to others and to causes greater than the self.

The authors remind readers that the human body did not evolve with the conveniences of the twenty-first century in mind. It evolved to adapt itself to the African savannah—to the cold, starvation, constant social contact, and daily hunting runs. For the first time in three billion years of evolution, humans have too much to eat and too little to do, and their primitive bodies are yet to adapt to this change.

Crowley and Lodge observe that, for the first time, people are living up to forty years into retirement. Now more than ever, there's every reason to strive to look and feel great for this third part of life. *Younger Next Year* offers a detailed look into the science of aging and the role exercise and engagement play in slowing down and reversing the normal aging curve.

PART ONE
TAKE CHARGE OF YOUR BODY

CHAPTER ONE: The End of the World

About 70 percent of all premature deaths (deaths before 80) are tied to poor lifestyle decisions. You can eliminate over 50 percent of the injuries and illnesses most people struggle with from the time they are sixty—sore joints, poor memory, and general body weakness—by changing your lifestyle.

If you exercise six days a week—lifting weights in two of those days—eat well, and commit to the people or causes you care about, you can subvert the "normal" aging curve and be younger in the areas that matter until you are eighty or older.

CHAPTER TWO: How's Your Wife?

As you get older, whoever you have in your life—your wife, close friend, or anyone you love—needs to be on your side. Life changes when you turn sixty or retire, and it's difficult to exercise, eat well, and commit on your own. Make a commitment to strengthen your relationships. Make plans to do things together.

CHAPTER THREE: The New Science of Aging

Aging is a slow and natural process characterized by graying hair, decelerating heart rate, and degenerating skin. Decay, which modern society has come to accept as synonymous with aging, is the dreadful wasting away of the body and mind.

In the absence of signals to grow, your body switches to the default, which is decay. You can prevent decay by overriding these default signals.

"The keys to overriding the decay code are daily exercise, emotional commitment, reasonable nutrition and a real engagement with living. But it starts with exercise." (p. 34).

The human body is designed to thrive in nature—specifically in the conditions of the African Savannah—not in the sedentary lifestyle or on the fast foods of the twenty-first century. Modern conveniences like temperature-controlled houses and abundant food have become a reality only in the last one hundred years. The human body, with its ancient physical systems, is yet to begin to adapt to these changes.

The physical brain has, for millions of years, interpreted idleness, excessive eating, and withdrawal from social contact as signals of approaching winter or famine. These behaviors—which are synonymous with American retirement—signal the body to waste away all but its essential functions—to grow old and decay.

Exercise triggers growth signals that spread throughout your body and mind. Social interactions and engagements send emotional messages that inhibit decay.

CHAPTER FOUR: Swimming Against the Tide

The Next Third of your life changes from a decay to a growth phase when you commit to serious exercise six days a week, every week, for the rest of your life. It changes when you make exercise your new job—when you take it seriously and make a big start from day one.

When you make it a routine, exercise that makes you strain and sweat sends growth signals that override the default decay process. It tells your physical brain not to turn you into an old senile mess.

Make a resolution to join a gym, at least for the group classes, the weight machines, and the weight training guides. Try a spinning or aerobics class, or any other kind of exercise class; it will give you the motivation and discipline to work out and help make exercise a habit. Make and stick to a schedule to reinforce the habit. If you have an athletic passion, make it your core activity. It will make everything easier.

CHAPTER FIVE: The Biology of Growth and Decay: Things that Go Bump in the Night

Your body is constantly destroying and renewing muscle cells, blood cells, bones—each of its parts—to adapt to new circumstances and create space for growth. Exercise sets off a chain reaction of inflammation that wears down and then rebuilds stronger muscles.

Only 20 percent of the blood in your body flows through your muscles when you are at rest. With constant exercise, as much as 80 percent of your blood flows through your muscles, carrying messenger proteins that initiate growth and repair to every part of your body.

You produce more of C-6—the chemicals for inflammation and decay—as you age, or as you sink into loneliness and chronic emotional stress. Exercise produces enough inflammation chemicals to trigger the production of C-10—the repair and growth chemicals. Exercise replaces inflammation signals with growth signals and reduces overall mortality.

CHAPTER SIX: Life Is an Endurance Event: Train for It

Devote four of the six days a week you exercise to serious aerobic exercise. Jogging, biking, speed walking—any steady exercise that elevates your heart rate will do. Start with six days a week of long and slow aerobic training to improve your blood circulation, clear the waste in your body, and flood your circulation with C-6 and C-10.

The key is to show up every day, do the day's work, and push yourself a little harder the following day. When you start, try to strike a balance between easy and hard so you don't get bored or strain so hard that you quit.

Consider taking up healing sports such as biking, swimming, rowing, or cross-country skiing.

CHAPTER SEVEN: The Biology of Exercise

Your body stores fat around your hips, belly, and a few other parts. Through your capillaries, it carries this fat to your muscles, which burn it for fuel. Aerobic exercises build more networks of capillaries, which increase the trickle of fat to the mitochondria in your muscles. Glucose is an alternative fuel source, but the body only burns it to give you the extra speed and power you need for hard exercise.

"Low-intensity, light aerobic exercise burns fat, while high-intensity, hard aerobic exercise burns glucose." (p. 100).

Light aerobic exercises are long and slow—think long hikes and bike rides. They are exercises that raise your heart rate to no more than 65 percent of its peak. They pull more blood to your muscles, which draw more fat from your blood. When prolonged, these exercises increase your circulatory and mitochondrial capacity and build endurance and general healthiness.

High-intensity exercises are exercises that raise your heart rate above 65 percent of its peak. These exercises—which burn fat in the background—draw glucose from the muscles for the extra energy. Hard exercises make you fitter.

CHAPTER EIGHT: The Heart of the Matter: Aerobics

A heart monitor helps you gauge the intensity of your exercise routines. Roughly, your maximum heart rate is the figure you get when you subtract your age from 220. If you are in good shape, you can get your real maximum rate by working out really hard for about sixty seconds.

Your target heart rate is 60-65 percent of your max rate for long and slow aerobic exercises, 70-85 percent of the max for high endurance, and 85-100 percent for anaerobic exercises. Your recovery rate—the beats your heart drops in the minute you go from peak performance to moderate exercise—indicates your aerobic fitness. Any recovery rate above 20 bpm means you are in good shape.

CHAPTER NINE: The Kedging Trick

It's easy to lose the psyche to work out six days a week until you die. To keep the motivation alive, set a desperate goal once in a while and push yourself to it.

Book a skiing, kayaking, or hiking trip—anything that forces you to train hard for months to handle it. Or pick up a challenging sport and make a commitment to get good at it. Whatever you choose, make sure it's serious and fun.

CHAPTER TEN: A World of Pain: Strength Training

Serious strength training two days a week, every week, does not just keep you healthy; it keeps you feeling good.

You lose bone and muscle mass as you get past age forty. Joints become brittle, the mechanisms that coordinate balance deteriorate, and simple movements become strenuous and painful. Strength training offsets bone and muscle loss and reverses the weakening of tendons and joints. Start early to skip a lot of the aches that come with aging.

Start with light weights and high reps to build muscle memory.

CHAPTER ELEVEN: The Biology of Strength Training

While aerobics build endurance, strength training builds muscles and increases the power they deliver. Strength training reverses nerve decay and, subsequently, improves coordination, increases joint and muscle strength, and keeps your reflexes strong.

Rigorous strength training—the kind that makes your muscles burn—secretes enough C-6 to trigger and flood your neural networks with C-10, the growth protein. It damages muscle cells at the cellular level and then builds new muscle mass in each cell.

Slow-twitch or endurance cells recover overnight, meaning you can do aerobic exercises every day. Fast-twitch or strength cells recover in forty-eight-hour cycles, so strength training should be limited to a maximum of three days a week.

CHAPTER TWELVE: The Ugly Stick and Other Curiosities

The changes that come with aging—the sagging skin, nose hairs, yellow teeth, thinning hair, and even grumpiness—are normal and inevitable. You can't change how you look when you age, but you can change how you feel by getting in shape, getting engaged, and eating right.

CHAPTER THIRTEEN: Chasing the Iron Bunny

Retirement changes your physical looks and your finances. You can get through the financial fog of retirement if you commit to spend less than you make.

Make a conservative estimate of your annual income and create a spending plan or talk to a stand-alone financial adviser. A good place to start is to quit pursuing the things you don't need. As long as you are above the poverty line, the status, power, or material things you add to your life will have a negligible effect on your happiness.

Live within your means and forget how it looks to the rest of the pack. They're over at the dump now, anyway, sniffing for fresh garbage. Look after yourself. On your own terms. And find a new pack. (p. 195).

CHAPTER FOURTEEN: Don't You Lose a Goddamn Pound!

A weight-loss goal is a fool's errand because 95 percent of all diets are unproven and certain to fail. Every food is complex, and scientists are only beginning to understand the millions of ways foods interact with and affect parts of the human body.

Exercising six days a week and eating healthy foods will get you in shape, no matter what you weigh. There's a good chance you'll lose several pounds while you are at it.

Ditch anything you know is bad for you, starting with all fast foods and processed snacks. Keep track of the calories you consume in meat, sugars, carbs, and drinks because they count. Ensure they are equal to or less than what you burn. A daily intake of 2000 calories for someone in his or her fifties or sixties is enough to maintain body weight. Fruits and vegetables are almost calorie-free, so stock up on greens. Limit your intake of carbs—including white rice, potatoes, and pasta—and saturated fat, red meat, and sugars.

CHAPTER FIFTEEN: The Biology of Nutrition: Thinner Next Year

The only way to lose weight is to avoid garbage food and go on a consistent and vigorous exercise program.

For thousands of years, sitting around was, to the human physical brain, a sign of impending famine—no matter the amount of food around. When you are sedentary, your Darwinian body takes it to be a sign of approaching winter/famine and uses everything you eat to build fat reserves. Exercise tells your body that it's still springtime and there's no need to build fat reserves. Springtime is a time to increase the metabolic rate and grow stronger and bigger, not fatter.

"The point of exercise is not to "burn off" calories, but rather to tell every part of your body to grow, to invest in building new tissue, and to run at a higher metabolic rate all day and all night long" (p. 216).

The Harvard food pyramid is a concise guide to healthy foods and servings. Get a copy of the pyramid and stick it on your refrigerator door.

If you have to eat copious amounts of anything, let it be fruits, vegetables, whole grains, and legumes. These foods are good sources of fiber and micronutrients. Go slow on salt and saturated fats.

Avoid starch from white rice, potatoes, refined flour products, and other white foods because it crashes your blood sugar and gives you the urge to keep eating. Your body knows when it has had enough of fats, proteins, and good carbohydrates such as whole grains and vegetables. It doesn't know when it has had enough of starch. White foods, which are basically sugar, initiate hyper-absorption and leave you feeling perpetually hungry.

CHAPTER SIXTEEN: "The Drink"

Taken in moderation, a drink or two a day—a drink being one and half ounces of liquor or five ounces of wine—can prevent heart attacks, strokes, and dementia. A little more than a drink or two also lowers the risk of heart attacks and strokes, but excessive drinking raises the risk of high blood pressure, diabetes, liver failure, and severe dementia.

PART TWO
TAKE CHARGE OF YOUR LIFE

CHAPTER SEVENTEEN: "Teddy Doesn't Care!"

It's tempting to not care about what you eat or what exercise you do, but it is the only way to get a decent body.

When you retire, it is not enough to care about exercise and nutrition. You have to care about people enough to reconnect and recommit to family, friends, companions, and community. You have to socialize like the Darwinian mammal you are or your limbic brain will trigger decay. Beyond that, you have to care about things above yourself—things like spirituality and acts of selflessness—to satisfy your essential human character.

CHAPTER EIGHTEEN: The Limbic Brain and the Biology of Emotion

For millions of years, survival depended on being part of a group. The limbic system, which runs emotions, synchronized the rhythms of early humans and enabled them to forage, hunt, and sleep with peace of mind.

Limbic resonance—the circle of emotions created by a group—moderates negative emotions and creates connections that feel good, both consciously and subconsciously.

When you isolate yourself, the reptilian brain—and its cascade of negative emotions such as fear, anger, and aggression—takes over. Your risk of depression, alcoholism, suicide, heart attack, and cancer increases, and your life expectancy plummets. It's the reason the life expectancy of married men is higher than that of single men. It's the reason Alcoholics Anonymous is so effective—it creates an instant community for people to connect and share emotions.

To reconnect with the people in your life, be there for them, share your feelings, listen, and play. Find a place to volunteer or a way to give back. It will strengthen your sense of belonging and of being needed, especially if you are retired.

CHAPTER NINETEEN: Connect and Commit

When you retire, you lose the pack of colleagues that you were part of. What keeps your connections alive is a project that reconnects you to your community.

Find something that taps into your passion—could be writing a book, running a community library or a hot dog stand, volunteering as an assistant coach at a school, or being a mentor—anything that gets you in contact with people. Use e-mail to reach out to old friends and find out if they have projects you can work on together. Humans, like rabbits and other mammals, thrive on contact.

Preferably, get a job that's different from the one you made a career out of. If you have an artistic side, tap into that.

CHAPTER TWENTY: Things That Go Bump in the Morning: The New Sexual Life

Testosterone and libido ebb in the Next Third. You will still have sex as much as you want, but you won't want it that much, and you will hardly notice that you don't want it as much as you used to. Except for that, your sexual life will be as fun and as intense as it used to be.

Men in their sixties and beyond have a significant risk of erectile dysfunction, but aerobic exercise can improve circulation and get them going.

Lack of interest is still normal. If your loss of sexual drive is due to a negative self-image, exercise can get you in shape and fix that.

CHAPTER TWENTY-ONE: Relentless Optimism

Every choice you make—whether to exercise or stay idle, eat junk or healthy food, connect or isolate—pushes you towards either growth or decay. Every day, you choose how you age.

The Next Third does not have to be grim or disconnected; it is bright for anyone willing to make harder choices.

KEY TAKEAWAYS

Key Takeaway: If you are not growing, you are decaying.

Decay is a default process the body falls back to when you stop moving and engaging.

For thousands of years, a sedentary lifestyle, especially among people past the childbearing age, signaled time to decay and make way for new generations. Even today, the default signals to decay get stronger each year past the forties and fifties.

Key Takeaway: Decay signals are all around.

The chronic stress of work and traffic, constant worry, loneliness, and other inconveniencies of the modern life triggers inflammation chemicals and, consequently, decay. Blood vessels carry these inflammation chemicals to every part of your body and expose you to the risk of several conditions associated with aging, including heart attack, stroke, hypertension, and even impotence. When you combine this stress with a sedentary lifestyle and dietary fat, you exacerbate your risk of chronic illnesses.

Key Takeaway: Exercise reverses decay.

Regular exercise inhibits decay because it is part of who you are; it is in your DNA, which has been passed down from ancestors who made daily sprints to hunt and forage. Physical exercise is a powerful signal that tells your body to grow—to strengthen bones and joints, increase oxygen and blood supply to muscles, and increase the immune function to handle the repetitive strain.

Key Takeaway: Make exercise your new job.

To make exercise your new job means to show up every day and do the work, without excuses or negotiations—until you die.

Commit to four days of long and slow aerobic exercises every week to burn fat and build endurance. The initial goal is forty-five minutes working out at an aerobic machine, swimming, or doing any exercise that raises your heart rate up to 60-65 percent of its max rate. Devote two days a week to serious strength training. Hire a trainer and aim for at least forty-five minutes of weight lifting.

Key Takeaway: Strength Training makes you stronger, fitter.

You lose muscle cells as you age. Strength training builds new muscle mass in the cells that remain. The implication is simple: you may lose half your muscle cells when you age, but it's possible to be stronger than you were when you were younger.

When you lift weights, rest for at least forty-eight hours to give your body time to repair your muscles.

Key Takeaway: Forget dieting; it doesn't work.

Your Darwinian body only knows two seasons: springtime—a time to build lean muscles and grow—and winter—a time to grow fatter and decay. It oscillates between these two seasons by the signals it receives from your physical and limbic brain, not from what you eat.

If you make garbage food and idleness a taboo, the excess weight will take care of itself.

Key Takeaway: Question the fitness lies and the excuses you make.

It's not aerobic exercise if it doesn't elevate your heart rate and make you sweat, and it's not working if—after months of exercise—you still have to catch your breath every few minutes. Walking to do some shopping does not count as exercise. Neither does playing a round of golf. Get a heart monitor to keep track of the intensity of your exercises.

You are never too tired to work out. You are only tired because you don't work out enough. A sedentary lifestyle drains you because the human body is not adapted to the modern humdrum of sitting idly or thinking all day. It is adapted for the African savannah—to run eight miles a day and endure bouts of starvation and other survival stresses.

Key Takeaway: Avoid refined carbohydrates.

The excessive sugar in white foods sends signals that get your body from thinking it has had too much to thinking it is starving in just a few hours. The havoc that copious amounts of sugar wreak in the digestive system is the source of numerous complications, including diabetes, heart disease, stroke, and even cancer.

It's easier to ditch sugar when you remind yourself that it is an acquired taste. It takes about a month to get used to sugarless coffee.

Key Takeaway: Connect and commit to live longer and happier.

For millions of years, being part of a tribe meant survival—it meant more food and more security. Even today, being part of a close-knit group that freely shares emotions increases your life expectancy.

When you connect with others, your limbic systems synchronize and you generate the positive emotions that make you feel complete. The brain lights up when you look at a face, more than it does when you look at things. The limbic brain is always looking to make a connection, always making emotional responses to the millions of cues it receives from the environment.

Key Takeaway: Love, compassion, and altruism enhance the immune function.

When you care, your limbic brain sends signals to the rest of your body that promote physical health and happiness. Studies have shown that people who do volunteer work at least once a week are two and a half times less likely to die than those who don't.

Key Takeaway: Examine your life to stay in control.

Keep a daily log of what you eat, what exercise you do, whom you connect with, and anything else you do.

Key Takeaway: Take a new job when you retire to stay engaged.

Retirement is the beginning of a new life, not a long vacation. There's immense satisfaction in work—even when you are old—especially when it's volunteer work. Get a job distinct from the one that made your career, or make one out of your hobby or passion.

Key Takeaway: Say "yes" to every request or suggestion.

It's tempting to decline suggestions to do things as you get older, but you need to get involved with other people, now more than ever.

Be the one who takes the initiative and suggests things—the one who makes plans for dinner parties, potato races, or cross-country ski tours.

EDITORIAL REVIEW

Chris Crowley and Henry S. Lodge's *Younger Next Year* is an exploration of the intricate science of health and aging and the commitments readers— especially those in their forties and beyond—can make to slow down their biological clocks.

The authors argue that the human body is in a constant cycle of growth and decay, the bias being towards decay for people past forty. A sedentary lifestyle, dietary sugar and fat, loneliness, and chronic stress invite decay, whereas exercise and engagement invite growth. They observe that most of what has been accepted as part of normal aging today—including weak joints, failing memory, slow reflexes, and the general deterioration of the body—is actually decay, which is optional.

Crowley and Lodge contend that it is that it is not so much what you eat that pushes you to decay; it is what you tell your physical and limbic brain with your actions and connections. It's either springtime, a time to increase the metabolic rate, build new tissue, and grow, or it's approaching winter, a time to stock up on fat, isolate, and brace for the impending decay. Crowley and Lodge assert that a "perpetual winter of sloth and gluttony" is responsible for at least 70 percent of the complications that lead to premature death.

Lodge—a practicing doctor who is board-certified in internal medicine and aging—digs into the science of aging and health and explains how growth and decay work. Crowley—a 70-year-old retired attorney and Lodge's star patient—offers the wisdom of his own experiences and a light and friendly look at all matters retirement.

Senescence, or biological aging, which *Younger Next Year* explores, has been a subject of interest for thousands of years. One modern school of thoughts has it that aging is programmed and follows a preset biological timetable, and the other has it that aging is the sum of environmental assaults on the body. The science Lodge uses to explain disease and aging draws from both theories, but largely from the damage or error theory of aging.

By the authors' admission, scientists are yet to completely understand how foods (and, in extension, other environmental factors) interact with and change the body. *Younger Next Year* only offers *one* of the numerous perspectives into what it takes to mitigate the detrimental effects of aging. Its biggest contribution is a detailed look into internal science—including how the body responds to growth and decay signals. This is not to say the book is ineffectual, because anyone who understands the *whys* will ultimately find and commit to the *hows*.

Beyond the simple advice to exercise, eat well, and connect with others, *Younger Next Year* does not offer any new ideas for becoming younger or fitter. The authors focus more on extolling the merits of exercise and interpersonal engagements than on exploring effective exercise routines, healthy diets, and practical ways to connect.

At their weakest, the authors dish out shallow advice such as "make a plan" to spend your retirement money wisely and "hire a trainer or read a book" to create the best strength training routine. Although this is a book primarily about the value of exercise and diet, the authors—it would seem—won't be bothered to recommend the exercise routines that work.

That aside, Crowley and Lodge put up a compelling case for taking up exercise, eating healthy foods, and connecting with people. They dig deep into the science of the muscles and mitochondria, the inflammation and growth chemicals, and the three human brains to postulate a theory of disease and aging that is as illuminating as it is gripping.

ABOUT THE AUTHORS

Chris Crowley is an American author and former litigator. Born in 1934, he retired early in 1990 to ski, bike, sail, and explore ways to stay fit and strong through the uncertain retirement years. Crowley has co-authored the *Younger Next Year* series with Lodge, including *Thinner Next Year* and *Younger Next Year, The Exercise Book*. His main focus is giving keynote talks on the aging revolution.

Henry S. Lodge M.D. is a leading New York internist and a Columbia Medical School Professor. His revolutionary insight—that humans remain hunters and gatherers at the core—has been the bedrock of the *Younger Next Year* series.

THE END

If you enjoyed this summary, please leave an honest review on Amazon.com…it'd mean a lot to us!

If you haven't already, we encourage you to purchase a copy of the original book.

A

*FAST*READS
PUBLICATION

34440723R00015

Made in the USA
Lexington, KY
22 March 2019